More French for Little Boys

A French workbook
for little boys

Written and Illustrated by: Yvonne Crawford

www.languageforlittlelearners.com

About this workbook

This book is a continuation of French for Little Boys. In this second level your son will continue his exploration of the French language while engaging in activities that will help to motivate him. He will design his own monster, make his own spaceship, open a sweet shop and much, much more.

This workbook is created especially for parents who do not have any prior knowledge of French. You and your son can embark on a journey of learning a foreign language together. Everything you need is inside this workbook, including a pronunciation guide, dictionary and teaching hints.

Every lesson will consist of a list of vocabulary words with pictures, three activities your son can do in the workbook with your guidance and two activities you can do together without the workbook for further practice. Each new word that is introduced will have its pronunciation next to it.

In the appendices there is a learning slide that he can color after he completes each lesson. This will help your child to see, and take pride in his progress.

Try not to put stress on your son to have perfect pronunciation or to remember every single word. If he forgets a word, simply repeat it and then use it in a sentence a few times; eventually he will catch on. It is important for him (and you) to have a positive first experience with learning a foreign language. It will encourage him to continue and succeed in the future with more language studies.

Table of Contents

Leçon 1

Ocean Creatures

Vocabulary:

la baleine *lah-bah-leh*
whale

la pouple *lah-pooh-pluh*
octopus

l'étoile de mer
lay-twahl-duh-mehr
starfish

le requin
luh-reh-kehn
shark

le crabe *luh-krahb*
crab

Fun Phrases:

oui	*wee*	yes
non	*noh*	no
peut-être	*puh-tehtr*	maybe

Teaching Tips:

- Throughout the day, ask your children questions in either French or English and then prompt them to answer you in French with the words they learned above for yes, no and maybe.

- If your child asks you what a word is in French that is not listed in this book, look it up in a French/English dictionary or on a website and then create a little dictionary for them out of a small spiral notebook. You can even have them draw the picture in order to help them to remember the word.

Activité Une

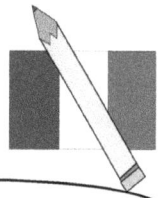

Bonjour! My name is Damien. It's nice to meet you. Can you match the picture of each ocean creature to its correct name?

la baleine

la pouple

l'étoile de mer

Activité Deux

Now you can greet each of my ocean friends in French! For each picture above greet the animal, say 'Bonjour', then say the name of the animal.

Activité Trois

Tell me which of these animals you like. If you like them write *oui,* and if you don't like them, write *non*.

J'aime... I like...

_____

_ _ _ _ _ _ _ _ _ _ _

_____

_ _ _ _ _ _ _ _ _ _ _

_____

_ _ _ _ _ _ _ _ _ _ _

_____

_ _ _ _ _ _ _ _ _ _ _

_____

_ _ _ _ _ _ _ _ _ _ _

_____

Activité Quatre

Your Very Own Aquarium

What you will need:

construction paper
crayons and/or markers
glitter
glue stick
scissors

What to do:
1. Draw a big aquarium on blue construction paper.
2. Draw ocean animals (or cut them out from magazines) and glue them to the aquarium.
3. Use crayons, markers and glitter to decorate the fish. Practice your colors in French as you color them.
4. Hang the finished aquarium on the fridge and every time you go to the fridge, point to the animals and say their names in French.

Activité Cinq

Starfish Toss

What you will need:

construction paper
scissors
pencil
cardboard
cap or cup

What to do:
1. Draw and cut out 10 starfish. You can trace the one from the workbook if you would like.
2. Glue them to pieces of cardboard.
3. Get your mother or father to help you cut them out.
4. Toss the starfish into the cap or cup and count them in French as you do. *une étoile de mer, deux étoiles de mer,* etc.

Leçon 2
Creepy Monster Faces

Vocabulary:

le visage *luh-vee-zahj*
face

les cheveux *lay-shuh-vuh*
hair

les yeux *lay-zyuh*
eyes

les oreilles
lay-zoh-ray
ears

le nez *luh-nay*
nose

la bouche *lah-boosh*
mouth

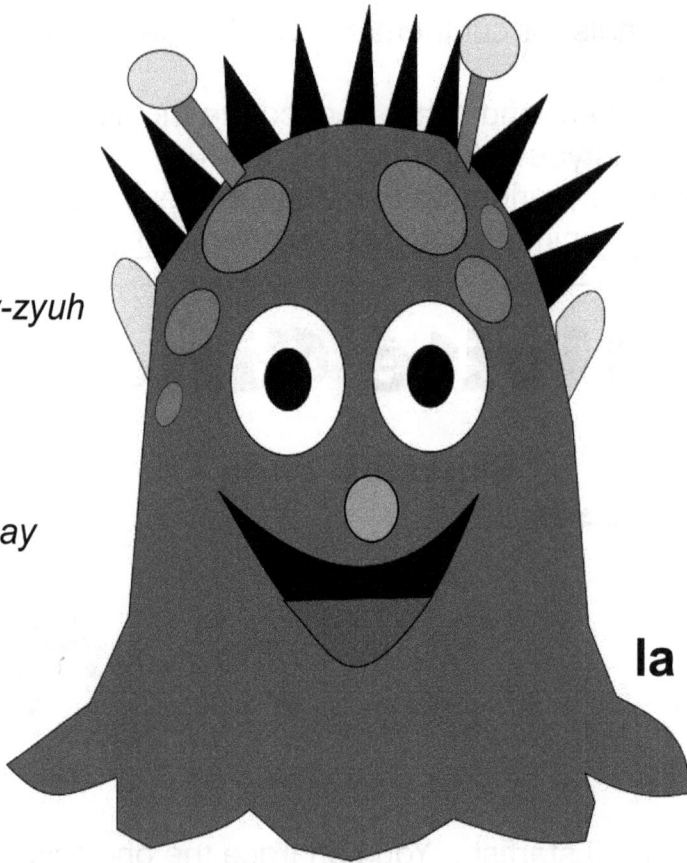

Fun Phrases:

j'ai peur	*zhay-puhr*	I'm scared
tu as peur	*too-ah-puhr*	you're scared
je n'ai pas peur	*zhuh-nay-pah-puhr*	I'm not scared
tu n'as pas peur	*too-nah-pah-puhr*	you're not scared
très	*trey*	very

Teaching Tips:

- Go through the lessons as fast or as slow as your child wants to go. Look to him for signs of fatigue. There is always tomorrow where you can take up where you left off today.

- Feel free to go back to the first level of French for Little Boys in case your son has forgotten things like colors or numbers in French. It's a good idea to go back and review earlier topics.

Activité Une

Come and meet my monster friends. Each of them is missing one part of their faces. Say the name of the facial part that is missing in French and then draw the missing parts on their face.

Activité Deux

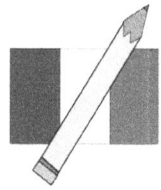

Oh no, one of my monster friends had to go away on vacation and he was supposed to spend the day with me. Can you draw me a monster friend? As you draw the different body and facial parts, say their names in French. Make sure to use colors and say their names in French too. Make the monster as scary as you want.

Activité Trois

This is Damien's favorite story about his adventure with a monster. Your mom or dad can read the story to you, and whenever you see a picture in the story, say the word in French.

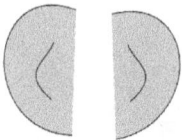

oreilles

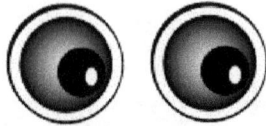

yeux

cheveux

bouche

nez

monstre

One day I was walking though the forest with my friend Pierre. I looked into the dark. I saw a   . However, I couldn't make out exactly what the   looked liked. I walked up closer to the   and I saw something that looked like huge light blue   . Looking even closer at him, I saw 2 round   . The   even had some purple spiky   . Who would've thought that a little creature like this would actually have some   . I even noticed that he had a rather round, orange   .

"Pierre?" I asked, "What do you think about this   ? Do you think that he is a good or bad?

"It's really hard to say," Pierre said. "Can you see his ⌐? "

"I think I can see his ⌐. He's smiling," Damien said.

"I have a flashlight, let's check him out to be sure," Pierre said.

Pierre pulled out a flashlight from his backpack and shined it on the monster. Both boys fell on the ground laughing. It wasn't a 👾. It was Damien's pet dog.

"Come here boy," Damien said, "You really had me going!"

"We really need to be careful about our imaginations getting the best of us!" Pierre said.

"Yeah, that sure was some 👾," Damien said, "Let's go home!"

Teaching Tips:

- Help your child create their own monster story. They can describe the facial features to you in French.

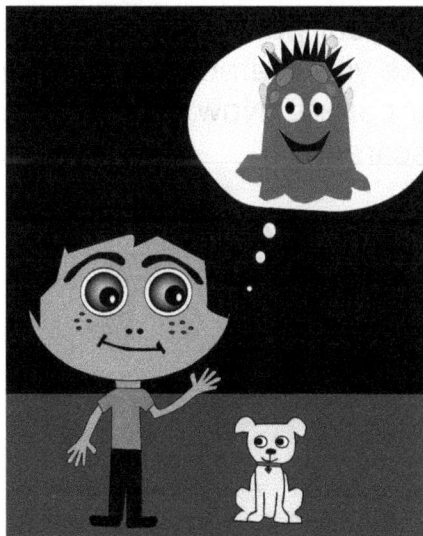

Activité Quatre

Yes, No, or Maybe?

Throughout the day, use your French whenever you can! When your mom or dad asks you a question, say the answer in French. Use: *oui*, *non*, or *peut-être*. Every time you say one of these words today, you can come back to this workbook and record it on this page. Color a star each time you use one of your new French words.

oui *non* *peut-être*

☆ ☆ ☆ ☆ ☆ ☆ ☆ ☆ ☆

Activité Cinq

Different Faces

What you will need:
your mom, dad or older sibling

What to do:
1. Your mom or dad will make a face.
2. In French describe how it makes you feel. Is it a scary face? Is it not a scary face? If the face your parent makes is scary say: *J'ai peur*. If the face does not make you scared, say: *Je n'ai pas peur*.
3. Switch roles with your parent. Now, it is your turn to try to make scary faces to make them scared.

Leçon 3

Out of this Worlds Numbers

Vocabulary:

l'extraterrestre
lehx-trah-tehr-ehs-truh
alien

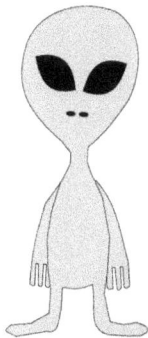

le vaisseau spatial
luh-vah-soh-spah-shee-ahl
spaceship

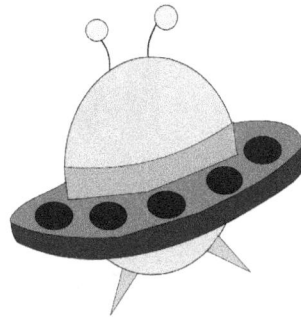

la planète
lah-plahn-eht
planet

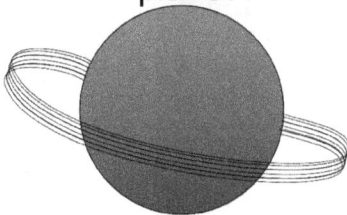

la lune *lah-loon*
moon

l'étoile
lay-twahl
star

la comète
lah-koh-meht
comet

11

onze *ohnz*
eleven

12

douze *dooz*
twelve

13

treize *trehz*
thirteen

14

quatorze *ka-tohrz*
fourteen

15

quinze *kahnz*
fifteen

Teaching Tips:

- It's easy for children to learn numbers in order. It is much more difficult for them to be able to say them out-of-order. Make sure you help your son practice his numbers both ways.

Activité Une

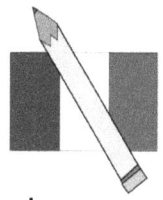

Count the different objects in French, then write the number in the box.

Activité Deux

Color the picture according the codes at the bottom of the page.

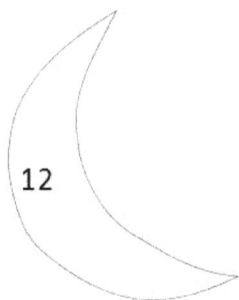

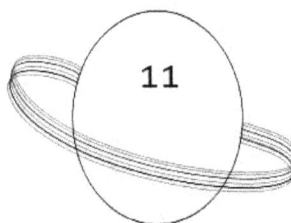

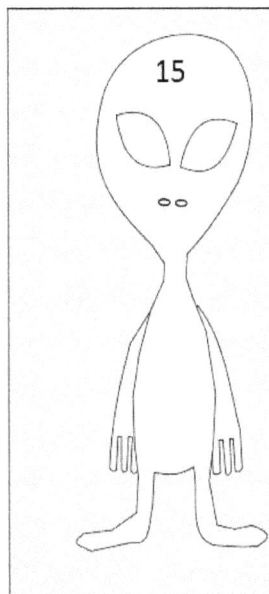

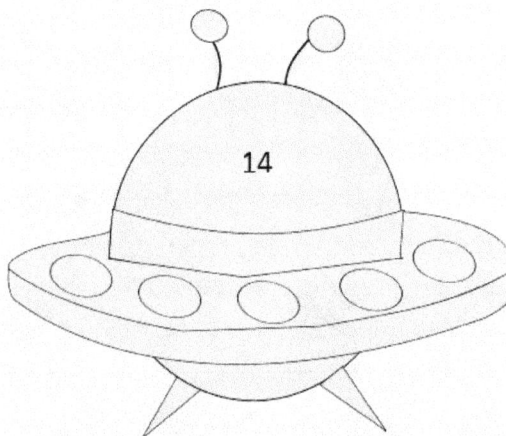

12

11

13

15

14

color key

onze - bleu   quatorze - noir

douze - vert   quinze - rouge

treize - orange

Activité Trois

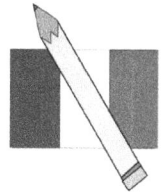

Match the number to the word in French. Then, write French number in the space provided.

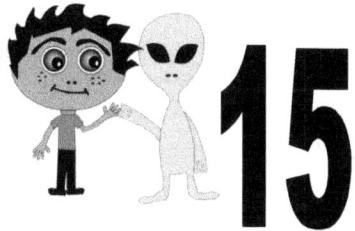

15

| douze | _ _ _ _ _ _ |

13

| quatorze | _ _ _ _ _ |

11

| treize | _ _ _ _ _ |

12

| quinze | _ _ _ _ _ |

14

| onze | _ _ _ _ _ |

Activité Quatre

Counting in Twos and Fives

Practice your French number by counting by twos, and fives. By doing this, you'll be able to remember all of the number more quickly. You can practice by counting your toys and grouping them first into sets of twos or fives. Have fun!

Activité Cinq

Make You Own Spaceship

What you will need:
an empty toilet paper roll
tin foil
construction paper or streamers
scissors
glue

What to do:
1. Wrap the empty toilet paper roll with tin foil, leaving a little extra on one side.
2. Twist the extra foil to make the point of the space ship.
3. Add streamers or strips of construction paper to the other side to be the fire of the spaceship.
4. Launch your space ship by counting down the numbers in French.

Leçon 4
Polite Pirates

Vocabulary:

le bateau de pirate
luh-bah-toh-duh-pee-raht
pirate ship

la carte de trésor
lah-kahrt-duh-tray-zohr
treasure map

le chapeau *luh-sha-poh*
hat

le pirate *luh-pee-raht*
pirate

le coffre de trésor
luh-koh-fr-duh-tray-zohr
treasure chest

l'épée *lay-pay*
sword

Fun Phrases:

enchanté	ahn-shahn-tay	nice to meet you
excusez-moi	ehks-kyoo-zay-mwah	excuse me
bon appétit	bohn-ap-pay-tee	have a good meal
à tes souhaits	a-tay-soo-ayt	bless you (said after a sneeze)

Activité Une

 Look at the pictures below. Draw a line from each picture to the correct phrase in French.

à tes souhaits

enchanté

bon appétit

26

Activité Deux

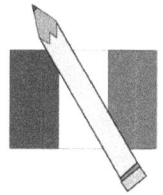

Look for the treasure chest at the end of this maze. As you pass each person on the maze, make sure you say *excusez-moi*, to be polite.

Activité Trois

Look at each picture below. Draw a line under your favorite pirate item and say the name in French. Next, draw a *orange* circle around your least favorite pirate item and say the name in French. Finally, draw a *bleu* circle around your mother's or father's favorite pirate item say its name in French.

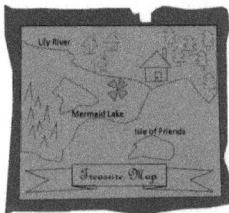

Activité Quatre

Arrrghhh I'm a Pirate

Dress up as a pirate and practice all of your favorite polite French phrases as a pirate. Say things like "*Arrrggghhh, bon appétit.*" before your afternoon snack. Be creative... if you don't have a pirate costume, use a bandana or a towel and tie it on your head like a pirate!

Have fun with this activity matey!

Activité Cinq

Pirate and Space Bingo

What you will need:
the bingo cards and calling cards from the appendix of this book
markers for the bingo cards - pennies or small stones
a hat or cap

What to do:
1. Your mother or father can cut the calling cards from the back of the book and put them inside a hat.
2. One by one they will draw one piece of paper from the hat and say the name in French.
3. Each time you hear a word, you look at your bingo card and try to find the picture. Place a marker on the spot if you have a match.
4. When you get five in a row, you win and you can shout out "BINGO!"
5. Try playing with a friend or a sibling and see who can win first!

BINGO!!!!!

BINGO

Leçon 5
Circus Fun

Vocabulary:

le cirque
luh-suhrk
circus

le dompteur de lions
luh-dohmp-toor-duh-lee-ohn
lion tamer

le clown
luh-kloon
clown

le monsieur loyal
luh-mohn-syuhr-loh-yahl
ringmaster

le funabule
luh-foon-ah-bool
tight-rope walker

seize *sehs* **16**
sixteen

dix-sept *dees-seht* **17**
seventeen

dix-huit **18**
dees-weet
eighteen

dix-neuf **19**
dees-neuhf
nineteen

vingt **20**
vahnt
twenty

Activité Une

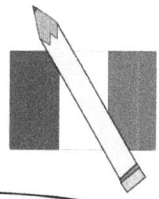

Bonjour! Take a look at the picture below. How many of my clown friends can you find? Try to find twelve. As you find each one, circle it in *rouge* and count each one in French.

Activité Deux

Use your crayon and connect all of the dots to finish his picture. As you connect the dots say each number in French!

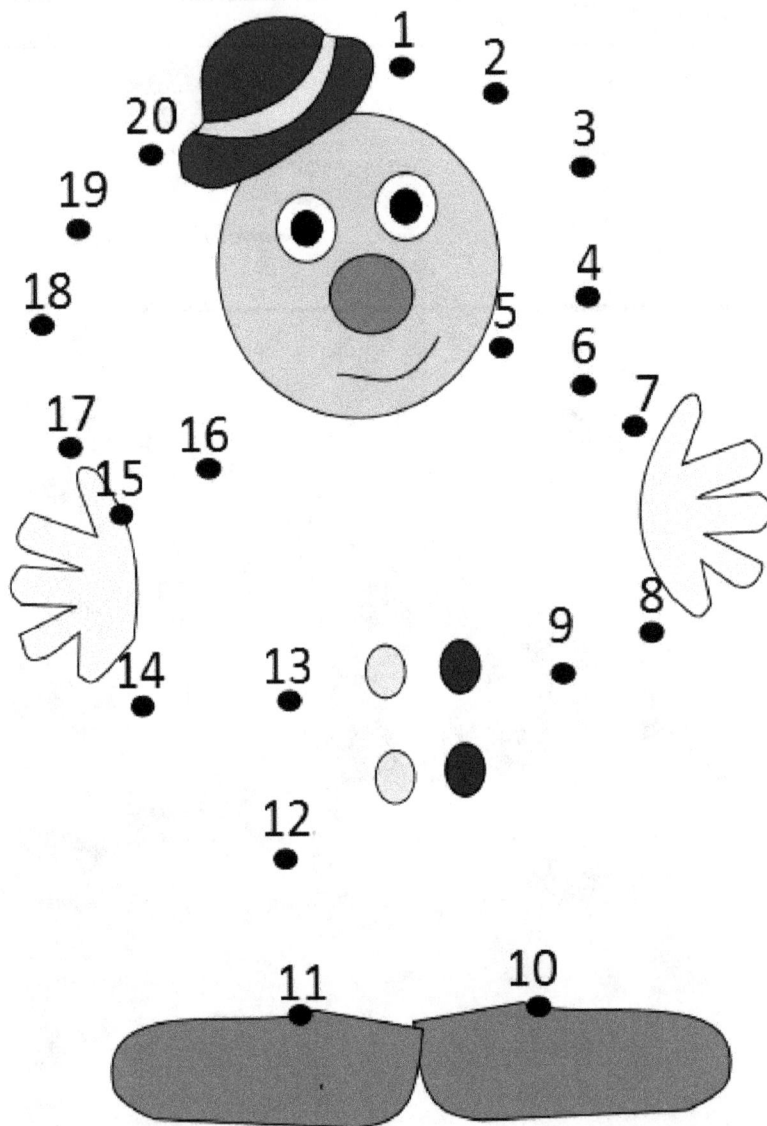

Activité Trois

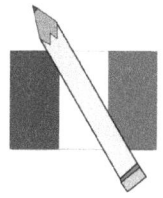

Count the pictures below in French, and then circle the correct number.

20	19	18

15	14	12

12	11	13

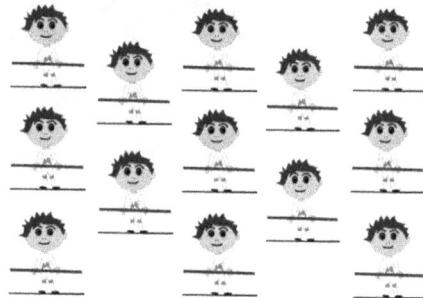

12	13	11

Challenge:

Start a collection of objects! Brainstorm with your parent about different things that could be in your collection (toy cars, rocks, sea shells, pencils, stamps, postcards). After gathering the objects for your collection, count the number of items in your collection in French. Try to find at least 20 items for your collection.

Activité Quatre

A Life-size Clown

What you will need:

freezer paper
pencil
markers or crayons
scissors

What to do:

1. Roll out enough freezer paper to lay on, and lay on it.
2. Have your mother or father draw an outline of you.
3. Now comes the fun part, turn yourself into a clown on the paper!
4. Draw and color clown clothes. Add big dots to the clothes and every time you draw one, count the dot in French. Try to draw at least 20 big dots on your paper clown.

Activité Cinq

A Dice Game

What you will need:

dice (3 or 4)
paper
pencil

What to do:

1. Roll the dice and count in French how many dots you have.
2. Let the next person roll the dice and then they will count how many dots they have in French. The person who has the most wins that round.
3. Write down on the piece of paper who won the round and keep playing until one person wins ten games.

Challenge:

Learn to count higher in French and play the game with 4 dice.
21- vingt-et-un   22 - vingt-deux   23 - vingt-trois   24 - vingt-quatre

Leçon 6

Sports Time

Vocabulary:

le football
luh-foot-bahl
soccer

le vélo *luh-vay-loh*
cycling

la natation
lah-nah-tah-seeohn
swimming

le golf *luh-gohlf*
golf

le basket
luh-bass-keht
basketball

le hockey sur glace
luh-haw-kee-suhr-glass
ice hockey

Fun Phrases:

je joue	*zhuh-zhoo*	I play
tu joues	*too-zhoo*	you play

Teaching Tips:

- When you say you play a sport, you need to put '*à*' in front of the sport's name.
- Please note that *à* + *le* = *au*.
- For some sports you need to use the verb '*faire*' instead of '*jouer*'. Then, you put '*de*' before the name of the sport.
- Please note that *de* + *le* = *du*.
- Here are some sentences to help you learn when to use which word:

Je joue au basket. - I play basketball.
Je joue au football. - I play soccer.
Je joue au golf. - I play golf.
Je joue au hockey sur glace. - I play ice hockey.

***

Je fais du vélo. - I bike.
Je fais de la natation or *Je nage*. - I swim.

Activité Une

Draw a line from the picture of the sport to the name of the sport in French.

	le basket
	le golf
	le hockey sur glace
	la natation
	le vélo

Activité Deux

Circle the six differences between the two pictures. As you find each difference count the number in French.

Activité Trois

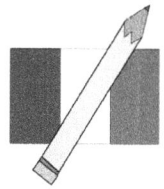

Answer the questions below about the sports that you play. Circle *oui* for yes and *non* for no.

1. Do you like to play "*basket*"?   Oui   Non

2. Have you ever played "*hockey sur glace*"?   Oui   Non

3. Do you like to "*faire du vélo*"?   Oui   Non

4. Do you "*golf*" with your father?   Oui   Non

Now, draw a picture of your favorite sport. If you know its name in French, write the name of the sport on the line below the picture frame.

Activité Quatre

Which Sports

What you will need:

a basketball
a baseball
a soccer ball
a bag

What to do:

1. Put all of the balls into the bag.
2. Pull out one ball and name the sport in French.
3. Repeat until you finish saying the names of the sports for each ball.

Challenge:

Add equipment from other sports and add it to your bag. Instead of looking at the objects, try to guess what each sport is by simply touching the object before you take it out of the bag.

Activité Cinq

Basketball Numbers

What you will need:

ten small balls
paper
tape
scissors
two hats or caps

(13)

What to do:

1. Cut out ten small pieces of paper and write one number on each piece of paper (11 to 20).
2. Tape one piece of paper to each ball.
3. Put all of the balls in one hat and put the other hat across the room.
4. Pull out one ball at a time and say the number in French, then throw the ball into the other hat. If you make it, you score a point. Good Luck!

Leçon 7

Sweet Shop

Vocabulary:

la barbe à papa
lah-bahrb-a-pah-pah
cotton candy

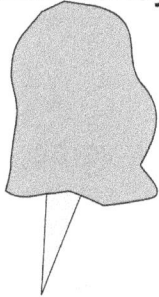

le gâteau *luh-gah-toh*
cake

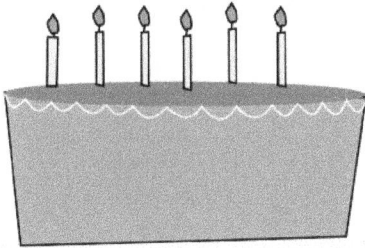

les boissons gazeuses
lay-bwah-sohn-ga-zuhz
soda pop

les bonbons
lay-bohn-bohn
candy

la sucette *lah-soo-seht*
lollypop

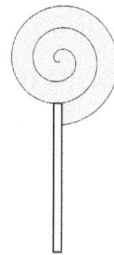

le biscuit
luh-bee-skwee
cookie

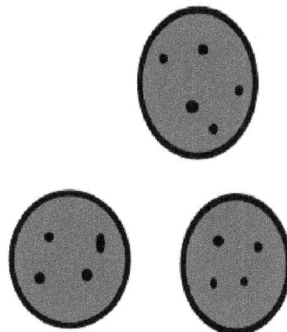

Fun Phrases:

je mange	*zhuh-mahnj*	I eat
tu manges	*too-mahnj*	you eat
je bois	*zhuh-bwah*	I drink
tu bois	*too-bwah*	you drink
je veux	*zhuh-vuh*	I want
tu veux	*too-vuh*	you want

Challenge:

- You can help your child form questions using the new verbs listed above:

    Qu'est-ce que tu veux manger? - What do you want to eat?

    Qu'est-ce que tu veux boire? - What do you want to drink?

- Remember to teach these lessons as slowly or as quickly as your child needs. If your child is not ready for this challenge, you can always come back to it at a later time.

Activité Une

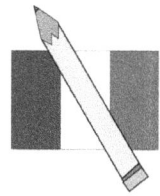

Look at all of the different *bonbons* there are to eat. Circle the *bonbon* that you think would taste the best. Then color all of the *bonbons* according to the color key below.

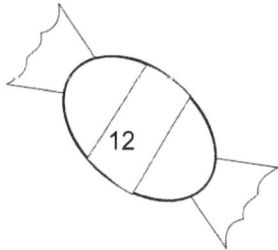

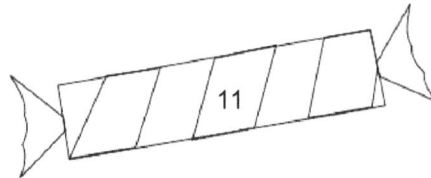

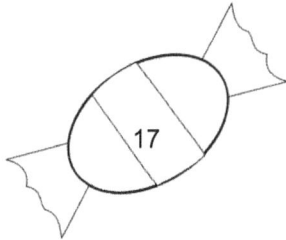

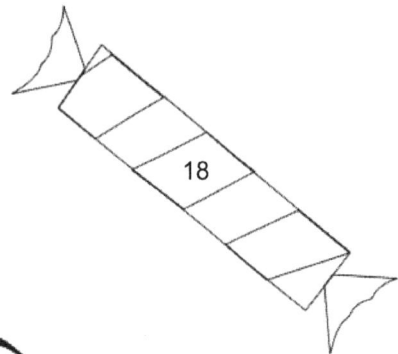

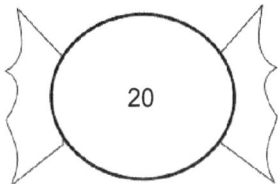

12

11

17

18

20

13

15

16

douze	rouge	onze	noir
dix-sept	blanc	**dix-huit**	bleu
treize	vert	**quinze**	orange
seize	noir	**vingt**	rouge

Activité Deux

Answer the questions by drawing a picture in the box below each question or circling the answer. (que or qu'=what; quelle=which)

1. Qu'est-ce que tu veux manger?

2. Qu'est-ce que tu veux boire?

3. Est-ce que tu veux un bonbon?   Oui   Non

4. Quelle bonbon?

Activité Trois

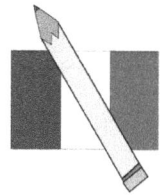

I need help filling these jars with bonbons. Draw the amount of bonbons listed under each jar. Thanks so much for helping me!

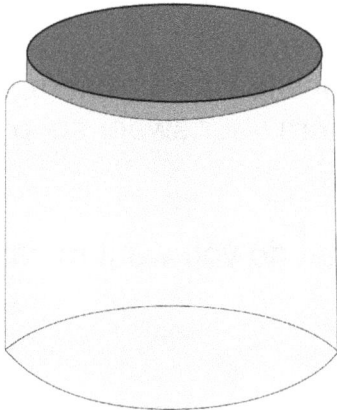

20

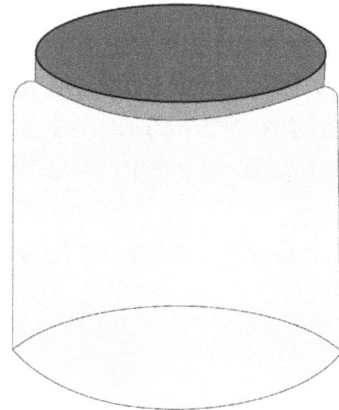

17

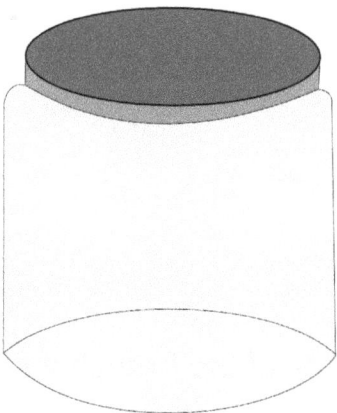

15

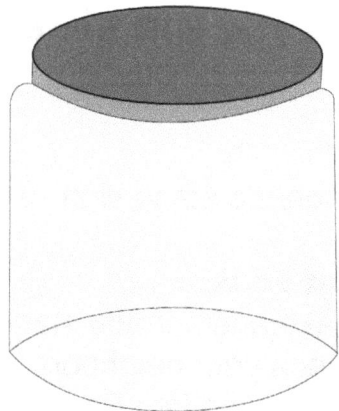

18

Activité Quatre

Your Own Sweet Shop

What you will need:

pictures of candy and sweets or blank paper
colors
scissors

What to do:

1. Either cut out from a magazine or draw your own pictures of sweets and candy.
2. Color and cut out the pictures that you've drawn.
3. Lay out all of your pictures on a table and invite your brothers, sisters and parents to come and pick out candy from your sweet shop.
4. You can say phrases like:

   Qu'est-ce que tu veux manger? - What do you want to eat?

Activité Cinq

Lemonade Stand

What you will need:

a pitcher of lemonade
cups
a table
a lemonade stand sign

What to do:

1. Make a lemonade stand in your front yard.
2. Teach your neighbors a little French. Use all of the French you've learned so far. Say things like:
   Bonjour - Hello
   Qu'est-ce que tu veux boire? - What do you want to drink?

Leçon 8
A Day at the Beach

Vocabulary:

la plage *lah-plahj*
beach

la ballon de plage
lah-ba-lohn-duh-plaj
beach ball

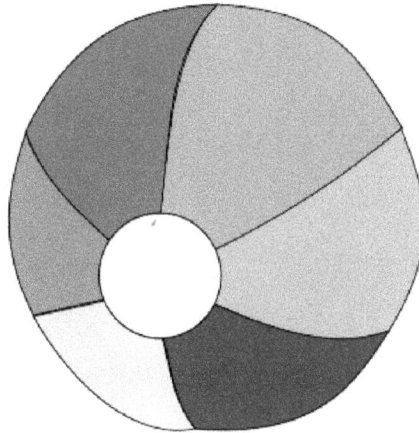

la mer
lah-mehr
sea

la coquille
lah-koh-keel
shell

les lunettes de soleil
lay-loo-neht-duh-soh-lay
sunglasses

le sable
luh-sah-bl
sand

le château de sable

luh-shah-toh-duh-sabl

sandcastle

Fun Phrases:

je nage	*zhuh-nahj*	I swim
tu nages	*too-nahj*	you swim

Teaching Tips:

- As your child learns new French vocabulary, try to have him remember the article with the noun.

  le - masculine or *la* - feminine

Activité Une

Come join me at the beach! Look at the picture and point to objects and say their names in French. Every time you say a name in French, then color the object.

Activité Deux

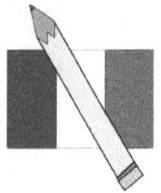

Draw a line from the phrase in English to the correct phrase in French. Then, draw a picture describing the phrase.

je nage

I swim

you swim

tu nages

I swim

you swim

Activité Trois

Draw a line from the picture to the correct word in French. Make sure to say the French word out loud as you are drawing the line.

la ballon de plage

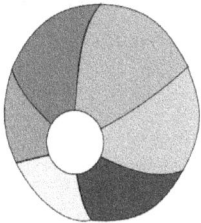

la coquille

la plage

le sable

la mer

Activité Quatre

Counting Coquilles

What you will need:
many coquilles or a trip to the beach
bucket

What to do:
Option 1:
Take a trip to a beach. Pick up as many shells as you can find and put them in your bucket. Every time you pick one up, count it in French.

Option 2:
Take all of the shells that you've collected before and give them to your parents. Let them hide the shells around your house or backyard. You can then search for the *coquilles*. Every time you find a shell count it in French.

Activité Cinq

A Sandy Picture

What you will need:
a little sand
paper
markers, crayons or paint
glue stick

What to do:
1. Make your own beach picture.
2. Draw all of the items that are listed in this lesson (get your parent to help you if you need help). As you draw each object, say its name in French.
3. Color all of the items in the picture, except the sand.
4. Rub the glue stick on the part of the picture that is sand.
5. Sprinkle sand on the glue and let dry.
6. Dust off remaining sand and hang up your picture. Every time you walk by your picture, point to the items and say their names in French.

Leçon 9
Race Cars

Vocabulary:

la voiture de course
lah-vwah-choor-duh-koors
race car

la voie de course
lah-vwah-duh-koors
race track

la ligne de départ
lah-leen-duh-day-pahr
starting line

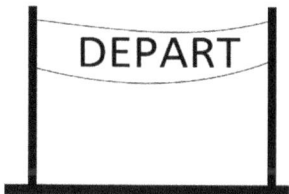

la course *lah-koors*
race

DEPART

la ligne d'arrivée
lah-leen-dah-ree-vay
finish line

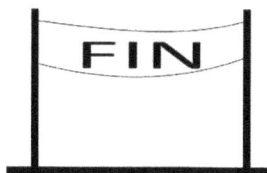

FIN

Fun Phrases:

j'ai gagné	*zhay-gah-nyay*	I won
tu as gagné	*too-ah-gah-nyay*	you won
j'ai perdu	*zhay-pehr-doo*	I lost
tu as perdu	*too-ah-pehr-doo*	you lost

Challenge:
It's fine for your son to memorize the past tense for the words above, but if you think he's ready for some grammar, you can introduce past tense in French. This is a very brief introduction of one past tense in French.

French has a few different past tenses. The one that is introduced in this lesson is called passé composé. Generally, it is used to describe an action that has been fully completed. *Passé composé* is formed by using one of 2 auxiliary verbs: *avoir* (to have) or *être* (to be). The verbs in this lesson use the first auxiliary verb, *avoir.* The auxiliary verb is conjugated in the present tense. Then, you put the action verb into the past participle. The past participle for win (*gagner*) is *gagné* and the past participle for lose (*perdre*) is *perdu.* Putting the two words together gives you the *passé composé.*

Activité Une

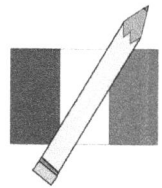

Look at the pictures of Damien. Do you think he has won or lost in each picture? Circle the correct phrase that you think he is saying for each picture.

| J'ai perdu. | J'ai gagné. |

| J'ai perdu. | J'ai gagné. |

| J'ai perdu. | J'ai gagné. |

Activité Deux

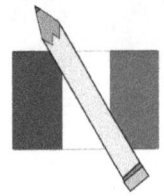

Who won the race? Trace the lines to figure out who really won. Then, on the line at the bottom of the page, write the name of the person who won the race.

Eva

Damien

Msx

_____ a gagné!

_____ won!

Activité Trois

Ask your mom or dad to help you read these questions. Then, circle if you won or lost each one.

The last time you ran with a friend, did you win or lose?

J'ai gagné.   j'ai perdu.

The last board game you played with your parents, did you win or lose?

J'ai gagné.   j'ai perdu.

The last video game you played, did you win or lose?

J'ai gagné.   j'ai perdu.

The last contest you entered, did you win or lose?

J'ai gagné.   j'ai perdu.

Activité Quatre

Playing Games

What you will need:
Any board or card game

What to do:
1. Play any board or card game that you have.
2. Try to use French as much as you can during the game.
3. At the end of the game make sure you use your new phrases: *j'ai perdu* and *j'ai gagné*.

> *J'ai gagné.*

Activité Cinq

A Speedy Car Race

What you will need:
toy cars
paper
masking tape

What to do:
1. Get your mom or dad to help you use masking tape on the carpet to make a race track (test a little area first to make sure that the tape doesn't damage the carpet).
2. Make a starting line and a finish line out of paper and put on the course.
3. Now it's time to start your engines!
4. Race your toy cars around and see which one wins. Make sure you use your French as you play on your *voie de course.*

Leçon 10

A Kingdom of Knights

Vocabulary:

le chevalier
luh-sheh-vah-lee-ay
knight

le château
luh-sha-toh
castle

le roi
luh-rwah
king

la reine
lah-rehn
queen

Activité Une

Can you please help the knight get to the *château*? As you pass each person in the maze, say their name in French.

Activité Deux

Color this picture according to the color key below.

le cheva-lier	bleu et noir
le château	gris
la reine	jaune
le roi	rouge et orange

Activité Trois

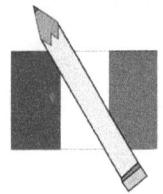

Fill in the missing letters and then draw a line from the picture to the correct French word.

le r__i

le che__ali__r

la re__n__

Activité Quatre

Matching Game

You will need:

the matching cards from the back of this workbook
scissors

What to do:

1. Turn the cards upside-down.
2. Turn over two at a time to see if you have a pair of the picture and the correct word in French.

Challenge:

Every time you make a match of cards, make a complete sentence with the word in French! For example:

Je mange les bonbons. - I eat the candies.

Activité Cinq

Pulling it Together

You will need:

any toys or objects that you have for which you learned French names in this workbook - stuffed sea animals, pirate hat, etc.
a backpack

What to do:

1. Put all of the toys and objects in your backpack.
2. Surprise your parents or grandparents. Tell them you have something to show them.
3. Then, one by one, take out each object and say their names in French. Try to make sentences too, if you would like to try.

Appendices

My Learning Slide

Every time you finish a leçon in the book,
color a section of the learning slide.

1
2
3
4
5
6
7
8
9
10

Three cheers for

_____

Félicitations!
Congratulations!
You have successfully finished
More French for Little Boys.

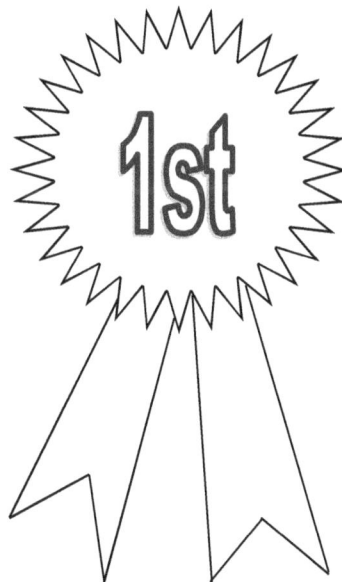

1st

English to French Dictionary

alien	l'extraterrestre	*lehx-trah-tehr-ehs-truh*
basketball	le basket	*luh-bass-keht*
beach	la plage	*lah-plahj*
beach ball	la ballon de plage	*lah-ba-lohn-duh-plaj*
bless you	à tes souhaits	*a-tay-soo-ayt*
cake	le gâteau	*luh-gah-toh*
candy	les bonbons	*lay-bohn-bohn*
castle	le château	*luh-sha-toh*
circus	le cirque	*luh-suhrk*
clown	le clown	*luh-kloon*
cookie	le biscuit	*luh-bee-skwee*
comet	la comète	*lah-koh-meht*
cotton candy	la barbe à papa	*lah-bahrb-a-pah-pah*

crab	le crabe	*luh-krahb*
cycling	le vélo	*luh-vay-loh*
ears	les oreilles	*lay-zoh-ray*
eighteen	dix-huit	*dees-weet*
eleven	onze	*ohnz*
excuse me	excusez-moi	*ehks-kyoo-zay-mwah*
eyes	les yeux	*lay-zyuh*
face	le visage	*luh-vee-zahj*
finish line	la ligne d'arrivée	*lah-leen-dah-ree-vay*
fifteen	quinze	*kahnz*
fourteen	quatorze	*ka-tohrz*
golf	le golf	*luh-gohlf*
hair	les cheveux	*lay-shuh-vuh*
hat	le chapeau	*luh-sha-poh*

have a good meal	bon appétit	*bohn-ap-pay-tee*
ice hockey	le hockey sur glace	*luh-haw-kee-suhr-glass*
I am scared	j'ai peur	*zhay-puhr*
I am not scared	je n'ai pas peur	*zhuh-nay-pah-puhr*
I drink	je bois	*zhuh-bwah*
I eat	je mange	*zhuh-mahnj*
I lost	j'ai perdu	*zhay-pehr-doo*
I play	je joue	*zhuh-zhoo*
I swim	je nage	*zhuh-nahj*
I want	je veux	*zhuh-vuh*
I won	j'ai gagné	*zhay-gah-nyay*
king	le roi	*luh-rwah*
knight	le chevalier	*luh-sheh-vah-lee-ay*
lion tamer	le dompteur de lions	*luh-dohmp-toor-duh-lee-ohn*

lollypop	la sucette	*lah-soo-seht*
maybe	peut-être	*puh-tehtr*
moon	la lune	*lah-loon*
mouth	la bouche	*lah-boosh*
no	non	*noh*
nose	le nez	*luh-nay*
nice to meet you	enchanté	*ahn-shahn-tay*
nineteen	dix-neuf	*dees-neuhf*
octopus	la pouple	*lah-pooh-pluh*
pirate	le pirate	*luh-pee-raht*
pirate ship	le bateau de pirate	*luh-bah-toh-duh-pee-raht*
planet	la planète	*lah-plahn-eht*
queen	la reine	*lah-rehn*
race	la course	*lah-koors*

race car	la voiture de course	*lah-vwah-choor-duh-koors*
race track	la voie de course	*lah-vwah-duh-koors*
ringmaster	le monsieur loyal	*luh-mohn-syuhr-loh-yahl*
sand	le sable	*luh-sah-bl*
sandcastle	le château de sa-ble	*luh-shah-toh-duh-sabl*
sea	la mer	*lah-mehr*
seventeen	dix-sept	*dees-seht*
shark	le requin	*luh-reh-kehn*
shell	la coquille	*lah-koh-keel*
sixteen	seize	*sehs*
soccer	le football	*luh-foot-bahl*
soda pop	les boissons gazeuses	*lay-bwah-sohn-ga-zuhz*
spaceship	le vaisseau spatial	*luh-vah-soh-spah-shee-ahl*
star	l'étoile	*lay-twahl*

starfish	l'étoile de mer	*lay-twahl-duh-mehr*
starting line	la ligne de départ	*lah-leen-duh-day-pahr*
sunglasses	les lunettes de soleil	*lay-loo-neht-duh-soh-lay*
swimming	la natation	*lah-nah-tah-seeohn*
sword	l'épée	*lay-pay*
tight-rope walker	le funabule	*luh-foon-ah-bool*
thirteen	treize	*trehz*
treasure chest	le coffre de trésor	*luh-koh-fr-duh-tray-zohr*
treasure map	la carte de trésor	*lah-kahrt-duh-tray-zohr*
twelve	douze	*dooz*
twenty	vingt	*vahnt*
very	très	*trey*
whale	la baleine	*lah-bah-leh*
yes	oui	*wee*

you're not scared	tu n'as pas peur	*too-nah-pah-puhr*
you're scared	tu as peur	*too-ah-puhr*
you drink	tu bois	*too-bwah*
you eat	tu manges	too-mahnj
you lost	tu as perdu	*too-ah-pehr-doo*
you play	tu joues	*too-zhoo*
you swim	tu nages	*too-nahj*
you want	tu veux	*too-vuh*
you won	tu as gagné	*too-ah-gah-nyay*

French to English Dictionary

à tes souhaits	*a-tay-soo-ayt*	bless you
la baleine	*lah-bah-leh*	whale
la ballon de plage	*lah-ba-lohn-duh-plaj*	beach ball
la barbe à papa	*lah-bahrb-a-pah-pah*	cotton candy
le basket	*luh-bass-keht*	basketball
le biscuit	*luh-bee-skwee*	cookie
les boissons gazeuses	*lay-bwah-sohn-ga-zuhz*	soda pop
bon appétit	*bohn-ap-pay-tee*	have a good meal
les bonbons	*lay-bohn-bohn*	candy
la bouch	*lah-boosh*	mouth
la carte de trésor	*lah-kahrt-duh-tray-zohr*	treasure map
le chapeau	*luh-sha-poh*	hat

le château	*luh-sha-toh*	castle
le château de sable	*luh-shah-toh-duh-sabl*	sand castle
le chevalier	*luh-sheh-vah-lee-ay*	knight
les cheveux	*lay-shuh-vuh*	hair
le cirque	*luh-suhrk*	circus
le clown	*luh-kloon*	clown
le coffre de trésor	*luh-koh-fr-duh-tray-zohr*	treasure chest
la comète	*lah-koh-meht*	comet
la coquille	*lah-koh-keel*	shell
le crabe	*luh-krahb*	crab
dix-huit	*dees-weet*	eighteen
dix-neuf	*dees-neuhf*	nineteen
dix-sept	*dees-seht*	seventeen

le dompteur de lions	*luh-dohmp-toor-duh-lee-ohn*	lion tamer
douze	*dooz*	twelve
enchanté	*ahn-shahn-tay*	nice to meet you
l'épée	*lay-pay*	sword
l'étoile	*lay-twahl*	star
l'étoile de mer	*lay-twahl-duh-mehr*	starfish
excusez-moi	*ehks-kyoo-zay-mwah*	excuse me
l'extraterrestre	*lehx-trah-tehr-ehs-truh*	alien
le football	*luh-foot-bahl*	soccer
le funabule	*luh-foon-ah-bool*	tight-rope walker
le gâteau	*luh-gah-toh*	cake
le golf	*luh-gohlf*	golf
le hockey sur glace	*luh-haw-kee-suhr-glass*	ice hockey

j'ai gagné	*zhay-gah-nyay*	I won
j'ai perdu	*zhay-pehr-doo*	I lost
j'ai peur	*zhay-puhr*	I'm scared
je bois	*zhuh-bwah*	I drink
je joue	*zhuh-zhoo*	I play
je mange	*zhuh-mahnj*	I eat
je nage	*zhuh-nahj*	I swim
je n'ai pas peur	*zhuh-nay-pah-puhr*	I am not scared
je veux	*zhuh-vuh*	I want
la ligne d'arrivée	*lah-leen-dah-ree-vay*	finish line
la ligne de départ	*lah-leen-duh-day-pahr*	starting line
les lunettes de soleil	*lay-loo-neht-duh-soh-lay*	sunglasses
la mer	*lah-mehr*	sea

le monsieur loyal	*luh-mohn-syuhr-loh-yahl*	ringmaster
la natation	*la-nah-tah-seeohn*	swimming
le nez	*luh-nay*	nose
non	*noh*	no
onze	*ohnz*	eleven
les oreilles	*lay-zoh-ray*	ears
oui	*wee*	yes
le pirate	*luh-pee-raht*	pirate
la plage	*lah-plahj*	beach
la planète	*lah-plahn-eht*	planet
la pouple	*lah-pooh-pluh*	octopus
quatorze	*ka-tohrz*	fourteen
quinze	*kahnz*	fifteen
la reine	*lah-rehn*	queen

le requin	*luh-reh-kehn*	shark
le roi	*luh-rwah*	king
seize	*sehs*	sixteen
la sucette	*lah-soo-seht*	lollypop
treize	*trehz*	thirteen
très	*trey*	very
tu as gagné	*too-ah-gah-nyay*	you won
tu as perdu	*too-ah-pehr-doo*	you lost
tu as peur	*too-ah-puhr*	you're scared
tu n'as pas peur	*too-nah-pah-puhr*	you're not scared
tu bois	*too-bwah*	you drink
tu joues	*too-zhoo*	you play
tu manges	*too-mahnj*	you eat
tu nages	*too-nahj*	you swim

tu veux	*too-vuh*	you want
le vaisseau spatial	*luh-vah-soh-spah-shee-ahl*	spaceship
le vélo	*luh-vay-loh*	cycling
vingt	*vahnt*	twenty
le visage	*luh-vee-zahj*	face
la voie de course	*lah-vwah-duh-koors*	race track
la voiture de course	*lah-vwah-choor-duh-koors*	race car
les yeux	*lay-zyuh*	eyes

Bingo

What you will need:

- Bingo cards – in this booklet.
- A hat or a cap.
- Something to cover up the squares on the cards, like dry beans or pennies.

What to do:

1. Cut out the cards on page 89, fold them and put them into a hat.
2. Draw one strip of paper out and say the word with the letter.
3. The children will cover up the word that they heard.
4. Repeat 4 and 5 until there is a winner!

B	I	N	G	O
		free square		

B	I	N	G	O
comet	star	sword	map	alien
pirate	ship	pirate hat	alien	pirate hat
treasure chest	alien	free square	comet	sword
sword	map	UFO	ship	map
UFO	pirate hat	pirate	star	treasure chest

B	I	N	G	O
sword	pirate hat	comet	map	ship
UFO	treasure chest	pirate	alien	sword
ship	star	free square	sword	alien
comet	ship	star	UFO	treasure chest
star	alien	map	pirate hat	pirate

Cards for Bingo

B - l'extraterrestre	B - le vaisseau spatial	B - la comète	B - l'étoile	B - le bateau de pirate
B - la carte de trésor	B - le chapeau	B - le pirate	B - le coffre de trésor	B - l'épée
I - l'extraterrestre	I - le vaisseau spatial	I - la comète	I - l'étoile	I - le bateau de pirate
I - la carte de trésor	I - le chapeau	I - le pirate	I - le coffre de trésor	I - l'épée
N - l'extraterrestre	N - le vaisseau spatial	N - la comète	N - l'étoile	N - le bateau de pirate
N - la carte de trésor	N - le chapeau	N - le pirate	N - le coffre de trésor	N - l'épée
G - l'extraterrestre	G - le vaisseau spatial	G - la comète	G - l'étoile	G - le bateau de pirate
G - la carte de trésor	G - le chapeau	G - le pirate	G - le coffre de trésor	G - l'épée
O - l'extraterrestre	O - le vaisseau spatial	O - la comète	O - l'étoile	O - le bateau de pirate
O - la carte de trésor	O - le chapeau	O - le pirate	O - le coffre de trésor	O - l'épée

Matching Game

What to do:

1. Cut out the following cards. Paste them onto card   board for stability if you would like.
2. Turn the cards upside-down.
3. Turn over two at a time to see if you have a pair of   the picture and the correct word in Spanish.

l'étoile de mer

le visage

le vaisseau spatial

la lune

le pirate

le coffre de trésor

le cirque

le football

les bonbons

la voiture
de course

le chevalier

www.ingramcontent.com/pod-product-compliance
Lightning Source LLC
Chambersburg PA
CBHW062106090426
42741CB00015B/3343

9780984454853